IMPORTANT INFORMATION
FOR MY FAMILY

End of life planning organizer.

Link to Companion Booklet
Important Information about my Funeral Plan

INTRODUCTION

Please note this book is not a last Will and Testament. Please consult a lawyer if you have not already done so. This book is designed as a useful guide for all the important information that your family will need in the event of your passing. It is not intended for complex trusts and businesses.

If you have a side hustle we recommend getting a second *Important Information for my Family* book and complete it for the business. It will be easier to keep the information separate as there could be multiple resources that need to be accessed for the small business.

If you chose to put sensitive information in this book, like passwords, please make sure you keep it in a safe place and let a loved know where to find it.

How to use this book

The pages on the left side, throughout the book, provides advice on how to fill out the information on the opposite, right hand page. We have included the most common details but everyone's situation is different. There is plenty of room to add notes where necessary.

To The Family

The information listed in this book is here to make your task simpler. A lot of the information you will need is contained in the following pages. We are truly sorry for your loss.

CONTENT

Personal notes to the family:

_____

_____

_____

_____

_____

_____

_____

_____

_____

_____

_____

_____

_____

_____

_____

_____

_____

_____

_____

_____

_____

_____

_____

_____

_____

_____

Personal notes to the family:

Personal notes to the family:

Notes:

CHECKLIST

Please google the requirements for your location as there will be regional differences. However this list should get you started in this trying time.

Things you will need to do:

Get Death Certificate and list the information here Agency: Date if Death: Registration Number:	
Tell friends and family	
Make arrangements with the Funeral Home	
Secure the property - houses and cars	
Throw out food	
Lock up valuables	
Provide care for pets	
Forward mail	
Notify Employer Ask if there is any outstanding pay Ask if there is any life insurance	
Find the will and contact the executor and/or lawyer	
Apply for grant of probate	
Open estate bank account	
Make an inventory of all assets (start with this book)	
List bills and cancel services (start wit this book)	
Notify banks and financial institutions	
Notify life insurance companies	

Continued on next page..

Notes

Continued from previous page

Notify Doctor	
Notify pension provider	
Notify financial advisors	
Notify accountant	
Notify credit agencies	
Contact tax advisor	
File final tax return	
Close credit card accounts	
Notify elections registrar	
Notify the Military (if applicable)	
Cancel driver's license	
Terminate insurance policies	
Cancel passports	
Cancel medical iinsurance, private and government	
Notify benefits provider	
Notify government services	
Notify Social Security	
Notify landlord	
Notify religious leader and place of worship	
Delete social media accounts	
Close email accounts	

Instructions for Completion

The first thing your family will need is your important personal information. If you have more than one passport then you can add the details in the "additional information" section

Notes

PERSONAL INFORMATION

Full Name: _____ Sex: _____

Maiden Name if applicable: _____

Date of Birth: _____ Race: _____

Place of Birth: _____ Certificate Nbr: _____

Usual place of Residence: _____

_____

Fathers Name: _____

Birthplace of Father: _____

Mothers Name: _____

Birthplace of Mother: _____

SSN/SIN: _____ Medical Card Number: _____

Veterans Discharge or claim number: _____

Marital Status: _____Name of Spouse: _____

Passport Country:_____Passport Number:_____

Organ Donor: _____

Additional Information:

_____

_____

_____

_____

_____

_____

_____

Instructions for Completion

Key Contacts are the first people that will need to be contacted. This is priority information, space for other contact information will be available throughout the book.

Notes

KEY CONTACTS

Next of Kin: _____
Phone Number: _____

Funeral Home: _____
Phone Number: _____

Executor: _____
Phone Number: _____

Lawyer/Attorney: _____
Phone Number: _____

Doctor/Primary Care: _____
Phone Number: _____

Employer: _____
Phone Number: _____
Phone Number: _____

Religious Leader: _____
Phone Number: _____

Accountant: _____
Phone Number: _____

Landlord: _____
Phone Number: _____

Alarm Company: _____
Phone Number: _____
Code: _____

This is priority contact information. Further contact information is detailed later in the book

Instructions for Completion

Your family may not have all the information for your friends and distant family members. You can list your contacts on the opposite pages.

Notes

FRIENDS AND FAMILY CONTACT INFORMATION

Name: _____

Relation to me: _____

Phone Number: _____

Name: _____

Relation to me: _____

Phone Number: _____

Name: _____

Relation to me: _____

Phone Number: _____

Name: _____

Relation to me: _____

Phone Number: _____

Name: _____

Relation to me: _____

Phone Number: _____

Notes:

FRIENDS AND FAMILY CONTACT INFORMATION

Name: _____

Relation to me: _____

Phone Number: _____

Name: _____

Relation to me: _____

Phone Number: _____

Name: _____

Relation to me: _____

Phone Number: _____

Name: _____

Relation to me: _____

Phone Number: _____

Name: _____

Relation to me: _____

Phone Number: _____

Notes:

FRIENDS AND FAMILY CONTACT INFORMATION

Name: _____

Relation to me: _____

Phone Number: _____

Name: _____

Relation to me: _____

Phone Number: _____

Name: _____

Relation to me: _____

Phone Number: _____

Name: _____

Relation to me: _____

Phone Number: _____

Name: _____

Relation to me: _____

Phone Number: _____

Notes:

FRIENDS AND FAMILY CONTACT INFORMATION

Name: _____

Relation to me: _____

Phone Number: _____

Name: _____

Relation to me: _____

Phone Number: _____

Name: _____

Relation to me: _____

Phone Number: _____

Name: _____

Relation to me: _____

Phone Number: _____

Name: _____

Relation to me: _____

Phone Number: _____

Instructions for Completion

Your family will need to be able to locate your important documents. It is sometimes best to put them in a central location. Please always make sure your documents are kept in a secure place. There is further space, later in the book, to list the location of other paperwork not listed here.

Notes

LOCATION OF IMPORTANT DOCUMENTS

Birth Certificate: ....

Will: ....

Power of Attorney: ....

Living Will: ....

Life Insurance Documents: ....

Passport: ....

SIN Card: ....

Medical Card: ....

Investment Documents: ....

Tax Records: ....

Property Deeds: ....

Vehicle Ownership Papers: ....

Marriage Certificates: ....

Divorce Certificate: ....

Business Records: ....

Phone and Address Book: ....

Password Logbook: ....

Instructions for Completion

If you have already made arrangements with a funeral home you can list the information here. It would be good to discuss this with your family ahead of time.

For a more compete funeral planning book look for the companion booklet *Important Information about my Funeral Plan,* also by Cadmus Collection. It can be found on Amazon, scan the QR code at the front of the book for a direct link.

Notes

FUNERAL HOME ARRANGEMENTS

Home Name: ---

Address: ---

Contact Name: --

Contact Phone Number: ---

Location of Documents: --

Details of Prepaid Services or Grave Marker:

_____

_____

_____

_____

_____

Wishes

_____

_____

_____

_____

_____

_____

_____

_____

_____

_____

_____

_____

Wishes

Wishes

Instructions for Completion

If you have a pet you will want to make sure it is taken care of by someone that will love them as much as you do. Talk to your designated person early to make sure they are
willing to take on the responsibility.

Notes

PETS

Emergency Caregiver: ....
Phone Number: ....

Vet Name: ....
Phone Number: ....

Documents Location: ....

Diet and Feeding: ....
....

Medication: ....

Allergies: ....

Grooming Provider: Address:..
....

Special Needs: ....

Additional Notes:

_____

_____

_____

_____

_____

_____

_____

_____

_____

_____

_____

Directions for Completion

If you are a property owner you can list your assets here.

Notes

PROPERTY ASSETS

Main Residence
Address: _____

_____

_____

Location of Deeds: _____
Location of Keys: _____

Secondary Residence
Address: _____

_____

_____

Location of Deeds: _____
Location of Keys: _____

Cottage/Cabin
Address: _____

_____

_____

Location of Deeds: _____
Location of Keys: _____

Notes

Directions for Completion

This space is for you to list your driveable assets. Things like:

- Cars and Trucks
- RV's
- Boats
- Bikes
- Off Road Vehicles
- Ski Doos
- Planes

There is space to list the storage location and keys. If there is separate storage address you can list this in the notes area along with the location of the storage keys.

Notes

VEHICLE ASSETS

Type of Asset: _____
Make/Model: _____
Year: _____
Plate: _____
Location of Asset: _____
Location of Registration: _____
Location of Keys: _____

Type of Asset: _____
Make/Model: _____
Year: _____
Plate: _____
Location of Asset: _____
Location of Registration: _____
Location of Keys: _____

Type of Asset: _____
Make/Model: _____
Year: _____
Plate: _____
Location of Asset: _____
Location of Registration: _____
Location of Keys: _____

Notes:

Notes:

VEHICLE ASSETS

Type of Asset: _____
Make/Model: _____
Year: _____
Plate: _____
Location of Asset: _____
Location of Registration: _____
Location of Keys: _____

Type of Asset: _____
Make/Model: _____
Year: _____
Plate: _____
Location of Asset: _____
Location of Registration: _____
Location of Keys: _____

Type of Asset: _____
Make/Model: _____
Year: _____
Plate: _____
Location of Asset: _____
Location of Registration: _____
Location of Keys: _____

Notes:

Notes:

VEHICLE ASSETS

Type of Asset: _____
Make/Model: _____
Year: _____
Plate: _____
Location of Asset: _____
Location of Registration: _____
Location of Keys: _____

Type of Asset: _____
Make/Model: _____
Year: _____
Plate: _____
Location of Asset: _____
Location of Registration: _____
Location of Keys: _____

Type of Asset: _____
Make/Model: _____
Year: _____
Plate: _____
Location of Asset: _____
Location of Registration: _____
Location of Keys: _____

Notes:

Directions for Completion

You probably have more assets than you realize. List any details of any safety deposit boxes, storage units and any valuables you may have around the house. If you are not comfortable listing valuables in your home make sure at least one other person knows of their existence.

Everyone's situation is different so there is space for other miscellaneous assets to be listed.

Notes

MISC ASSETS

Safety Deposit Box

Location:

Content:

Access
Details:

Rental Unit

Location:

Content:

Access
Details:

Valuables in the House

Location or details of the person who knows the location:

Notes:

OTHER ASSETS

Type of Asset:	
Location of Asset:	
Notes:	

Type of Asset:	
Location of Asset:	
Notes:	

Type of Asset:	
Location of Asset:	
Notes:	

Notes:

OTHER ASSETS

Type of Asset:	
Location of Asset:	
Notes:	

Type of Asset:	
Location of Asset:	
Notes:	

Type of Asset:	
Location of Asset:	
Notes:	

Directions for Completion

Most of us have multiple daily bank accounts. Whether they are checking/chequing accounts or savings accounts. Make sure your family knows about them all, across all financial institutions. There is a separate space for listing investment accounts/vehicles.

Notes

DAILY BANK ACCOUNT INFO

Banking Institution: _____
Location: _____
Account Type: _____
Account Number: _____
Approx Value: _____
Internet User Name: _____
Password: _____

Banking Institution: _____
Location: _____
Account Type: _____
Account Number: _____
Approx Value: _____
Internet User Name _____
Password: _____

Banking Institution: _____
Location: _____
Account Type: _____
Account Number: _____
Approx Value: _____
Internet User Name: _____
Password: _____

Banking Institution: _____
Location: _____
Account Type: _____
Account Number: _____
Approx Value: _____
Internet User Name: _____
Password: _____

Notes:

DAILY BANK ACCOUNT INFO

Banking Institution: _____
Location: _____
Account Type: _____
Account Number: _____
Approx Value: _____
Internet User Name: _____
Password: _____

Banking Institution: _____
Location: _____
Account Type: _____
Account Number: _____
Approx Value: _____
Internet User Name _____
Password: _____

Banking Institution: _____
Location: _____
Account Type: _____
Account Number: _____
Approx Value: _____
Internet User Name: _____
Password: _____

Banking Institution: _____
Location: _____
Account Type: _____
Account Number: _____
Approx Value: _____
Internet User Name: _____
Password: _____

Directions for Completion

We will now continue to list your financial assets. If you use a financial planner you can list their contact information here. You can also list any other investments like stocks, bitcoin or online investments.

Notes

INVESTMENT ACCOUNT INFORMATION

Financial Planner: _____

Address: _____

_____

_____

Email: _____

Phone Number: _____

Institution/Trading Platform: _____

Type of Investment: _____

Account Number: _____

Approx $: _____

Internet Username: _____

Password: _____

Institution/Trading Platform: _____

Type of Investment: _____

Account Number: _____

Approx $: _____

Internet Username: _____

Password: _____

Institution/Trading Platform: _____

Type of Investment: _____

Account Number: _____

Approx $: _____

Internet Username: _____

Password: _____

Notes:

Institution/Trading Platform: _____
Type of Investment: _____
Account Number: _____
Approx $: _____
Internet Username: _____
Password: _____

Institution/Trading Platform: _____
Type of Investment: _____
Account Number: _____
Approx $: _____
Internet Username: _____
Password: _____

Institution/Trading Platform: _____
Type of Investment: _____
Account Number: _____
Approx $: _____
Internet Username: _____
Password: _____

Institution/Trading Platform: _____
Type of Investment: _____
Account Number: _____
Approx $: _____
Internet Username: _____
Password: _____

Notes:

Institution/Trading Platform: _____
Type of Investment: _____
Account Number: _____
Approx $: _____
Internet Username: _____
Password: _____

Institution/Trading Platform: _____
Type of Investment: _____
Account Number: _____
Approx $: _____
Internet Username: _____
Password: _____

Institution/Trading Platform: _____
Type of Investment: _____
Account Number: _____
Approx $: _____
Internet Username: _____
Password: _____

Institution/Trading Platform: _____
Type of Investment: _____
Account Number: _____
Approx $: _____
Internet Username: _____
Password: _____

Instructions for Completion

If you have specific retirement vehicles like annuities, pensions, military benefits or government benefits you can list them here

Notes

RETIREMENT ASSETS

PENSION	
Company	
Contact Info	
Acc. Number	
Docs Location	

PENSION	
Company	
Contact Info	
Acc. Number	
Docs Location	

Notes:

Notes:

ANNUITY	
Company	
Contact Info	
Acc. Number	
Docs Location	

ANNUITY	
Company	
Contact Info	
Acc. Number	
Docs Location	

Notes

Notes:

MILITARY BENEFITS

Contact Info	
ID Number	

Notes

GOVERNMENT BENEFITS

Contact Info	
ID Number	

Notes

Directions for Completion

This space is for you to list all of your loans and debts. These could be personal loans, lines of credit, mortgages or credit cards.

Notes

LOAN and DEBT INFORMATION

Lender:
Location of Docs:
Loan Type:
Account Number:
Approx Owed:
Internet Username:
Password:

Lender:
Location of Docs:
Loan Type:
Account Number:
Approx Owed:
Internet Username:
Password:

Lender:
Location of Docs:
Loan Type:
Account Number:
Approx Owed:
Internet Username:
Password:

Lender:
Location of Docs:
Loan Type:
Account Number:
Approx Owed:
Internet Username:
Password:

Notes:

LOAN and DEBT INFORMATION

Lender: ....
Location of Docs: ....
Loan Type: ....
Account Number: ....
Approx Owed: ....
Internet Username: ....
Password: ....

Lender: ....
Location of Docs: ....
Loan Type: ....
Account Number: ....
Approx Owed: ....
Internet Username: ....
Password: ....

Lender: ....
Location of Docs: ....
Loan Type: ....
Account Number: ....
Approx Owed: ....
Internet Username: ....
Password: ....

Lender: ....
Location of Docs: ....
Loan Type: ....
Account Number: ....
Approx Owed: ....
Internet Username: ....
Password: ....

Notes:

LOAN and DEBT INFORMATION

Lender: ....
Location of Docs: ....
Loan Type: ....
Account Number: ....
Approx Owed: ....
Internet Username: ....
Password: ....

Lender: ....
Location of Docs: ....
Loan Type: ....
Account Number: ....
Approx Owed: ....
Internet Username: ....
Password: ....

Lender: ....
Location of Docs: ....
Loan Type: ....
Account Number: ....
Approx Owed: ....
Internet Username: ....
Password: ....

Lender: ....
Location of Docs: ....
Loan Type: ....
Account Number: ....
Approx Owed: ....
Internet Username: ....
Password: ....

Directions for Completion

We can have a lot of insurance that covers us personally. These can include

- Life Insurance
- Accidental Death and Dismemberment
- Critical Illness
- Workers Compensation
- Veterans Funeral Expense

Among others. Some may have been purchased specifically others may have been made available through your employer, union or association, or credit card. Make sure your family claims everything to which they are entitled

Notes

PERSONAL INSURANCE

Type	
Provider	
Contact Info	
Policy Number	
Location of Policy	

Type	
Provider	
Contact Info	
Policy Number	
Location of Policy	

Type	
Provider	
Contact Info	
Policy Number	
Location of Policy	

Notes

PERSONAL INSURANCE cont.d

Type	
Provider	
Contact Info	
Policy Number	
Location of Policy	

Type	
Provider	
Contact Info	
Policy Number	
Location of Policy	

Type	
Provider	
Contact Info	
Policy Number	
Location of Policy	

Notes

PERSONAL INSURANCE cont.d

Type	
Provider	
Contact Info	
Policy Number	
Location of Policy	

Type	
Provider	
Contact Info	
Policy Number	
Location of Policy	

Type	
Provider	
Contact Info	
Policy Number	
Location of Policy	

Directions for Completion

You will probably have other insurance that will need to be cancelled when your assets are transferred to a family member or sold.

This type of Insurance will cover things like
- Home
- Auto
- Renters
- Health

This is not an exhaustive list, each circumstance will be different.

Notes

ITEM INSURANCE

Insurance Type	
Item Covered	
Provider	
Contact Info	
Policy Number	
Value	
Policy Location	
Notes	

Insurance Type	
Item Covered	
Provider	
Contact Info	
Policy Number	
Value	
Policy Location	
Notes	

Notes

ITEM INSURANCE

Insurance Type	
Item Covered	
Provider	
Contact Info	
Policy Number	
Value	
Policy Location	
Notes	

Insurance Type	
Item Covered	
Provider	
Contact Info	
Policy Number	
Value	
Policy Location	
Notes	

Notes

ITEM INSURANCE

Insurance Type	
Item Covered	
Provider	
Contact Info	
Policy Number	
Value	
Policy Location	
Notes	

Insurance Type	
Item Covered	
Provider	
Contact Info	
Policy Number	
Value	
Policy Location	
Notes	

Notes

ITEM INSURANCE

Insurance Type	
Item Covered	
Provider	
Contact Info	
Policy Number	
Value	
Policy Location	
Notes	

Insurance Type	
Item Covered	
Provider	
Contact Info	
Policy Number	
Value	
Policy Location	
Notes	

Directions for Completion

There will be many household bills and regular billing that will need to be cancelled. Apart from the obvious things like gas and electricity there are bills like streaming services, for example Netflix. A lot of these services do not send a bill and your family will not know which services you subscribe to unless you list them. Following is a list to remind you of your possible bills, it is not an exhaustive list but should lead you in the right direction

- House Taxes
- Gas
- Electricity
- Utilities
- Cable
- Internet
- Phone
- Cell Phone
- Netflix
- Amazon Prime
- Apple TV
- Alarm

Notes

HOUSEHOLD AND RECURRING BILLS

Bill Name: ....
Provider: ....
Cost: ....
Payment Frequency: ....
Autopay: YES/NO
If yes, account paid from: ....

Bill Name: ....
Provider: ....
Cost: ....
Payment Frequency: ....
Autopay: YES/NO
If yes, account paid from: ....

Bill Name: ....
Provider: ....
Cost: ....
Payment Frequency: ....
Autopay: YES/NO
If yes, account paid from: ....

Bill Name: ....
Provider: ....
Cost: ....
Payment Frequency: ....
Autopay: YES/NO
If yes, account paid from: ....

Notes

HOUSEHOLD AND RECURRING BILLS

Bill Name: _____
Provider: _____
Cost: _____
Payment Frequency: _____
Autopay: YES/NO
If yes, account paid from: _____

Bill Name: _____
Provider: _____
Cost: _____
Payment Frequency: _____
Autopay: YES/NO
If yes, account paid from: _____

Bill Name: _____
Provider: _____
Cost: _____
Payment Frequency: _____
Autopay: YES/NO
If yes, account paid from: _____

Bill Name: _____
Provider: _____
Cost: _____
Payment Frequency: _____
Autopay: YES/NO
If yes, account paid from: _____

Notes

HOUSEHOLD AND RECURRING BILLS

Bill Name: _____
Provider: _____
Cost: _____
Payment Frequency: _____
Autopay: YES/NO
If yes, account paid from: _____

Bill Name: _____
Provider: _____
Cost: _____
Payment Frequency: _____
Autopay: YES/NO
If yes, account paid from: _____

Bill Name: _____
Provider: _____
Cost: _____
Payment Frequency: _____
Autopay: YES/NO
If yes, account paid from: _____

Bill Name: _____
Provider: _____
Cost: _____
Payment Frequency: _____
Autopay: YES/NO
If yes, account paid from: _____

Notes

HOUSEHOLD AND RECURRING BILLS

Bill Name: _____
Provider: _____
Cost: _____
Payment Frequency: _____
Autopay: YES/NO
If yes, account paid from: _____

Bill Name: _____
Provider: _____
Cost: _____
Payment Frequency: _____
Autopay: YES/NO
If yes, account paid from: _____

Bill Name: _____
Provider: _____
Cost: _____
Payment Frequency: _____
Autopay: YES/NO
If yes, account paid from: _____

Bill Name: _____
Provider: _____
Cost: _____
Payment Frequency: _____
Autopay: YES/NO
If yes, account paid from: _____

Notes

HOUSEHOLD AND RECURRING BILLS

Bill Name: _____
Provider: _____
Cost: _____
Payment Frequency: _____
Autopay: YES/NO
If yes, account paid from: _____

Bill Name: _____
Provider: _____
Cost: _____
Payment Frequency: _____
Autopay: YES/NO
If yes, account paid from: _____

Bill Name: _____
Provider: _____
Cost: _____
Payment Frequency: _____
Autopay: YES/NO
If yes, account paid from: _____

Bill Name: _____
Provider: _____
Cost: _____
Payment Frequency: _____
Autopay: YES/NO
If yes, account paid from: _____

Notes

HOUSEHOLD AND RECURRING BILLS

Bill Name: ....
Provider: ....
Cost: ....
Payment Frequency: ....
Autopay: YES/NO
If yes, account paid from: ....

Bill Name: ....
Provider: ....
Cost: ....
Payment Frequency: ....
Autopay: YES/NO
If yes, account paid from: ....

Bill Name: ....
Provider: ....
Cost: ....
Payment Frequency: ....
Autopay: YES/NO
If yes, account paid from: ....

Bill Name: ....
Provider: ....
Cost: ....
Payment Frequency: ....
Autopay: YES/NO
If yes, account paid from: ....

Directions for Completion

If you have any other memberships or regular donations to any organizations you can list them here.

Don't forget large organizations like Roadside Assistance membership as well as smaller organizations like the Golf or sports club, or the Gym or Yoga studio.

Notes

MEMBERSHIPS AND ORGANIZATIONS

Organization	
Dues	
Member Number	
Contact Info	
Notes	

Organization	
Dues	
Member Number	
Contact Info	
Notes	

Organization	
Dues	
Member Number	
Contact Info	
Notes	

Notes

MEMBERSHIPS AND ORGANIZATIONS

Organization	
Dues	
Member Number	
Contact Info	
Notes	

Organization	
Dues	
Member Number	
Contact Info	
Notes	

Organization	
Dues	
Member Number	
Contact Info	
Notes	

Notes

MEMBERSHIPS AND ORGANIZATIONS

Organization	
Dues	
Member Number	
Contact Info	
Notes	

Organization	
Dues	
Member Number	
Contact Info	
Notes	

Organization	
Dues	
Member Number	
Contact Info	
Notes	

Directions for Completion

Nearly all electronic devices require a password to gain access. Chances are you have at least a couple of these. If you have a computer, ipad or cell phone then you will need to list the access codes to these devices so your family can gain access to them, not only to gain valuable information but also so they can use them in the future.

Notes

DEVICE PASSWORDS

Type of Device	
Usual Location	
Password	

Type of Device	
Usual Location	
Password	

Type of Device	
Usual Location	
Password	

Type of Device	
Usual Location	
Password	

Type of Device	
Usual Location	
Password	

Directions for Completion

Although your electronic devices can remember your usernames and passwords it is best to have them listed so your family can gain access to different websites from any computer. If you have a separate password logbook you can advise of its location under "Location of Important Documents"

These websites could be for online billing of previously listed "Household and Recurring Bills" or other websites you visit regularly. Don't forget information for travel websites like Airlines, Hotels and Rental Cars. There may be points that the family can use.

The same goes for other loyalty points like Airmiles and grocery stores.

Notes

WEBSITE PASSWORDS

Website	
User Name	
Password	

Website	
User Name	
Password	

Website	
User Name	
Password	

Website	
User Name	
Password	

Website	
User Name	
Password	

Notes

WEBSITE PASSWORDS

Website	
User Name	
Password	

Website	
User Name	
Password	

Website	
User Name	
Password	

Website	
User Name	
Password	

Website	
User Name	
Password	

Notes

WEBSITE PASSWORDS

Website	
User Name	
Password	

Website	
User Name	
Password	

Website	
User Name	
Password	

Website	
User Name	
Password	

Website	
User Name	
Password	

Notes

WEBSITE PASSWORDS

Website	
User Name	
Password	

Website	
User Name	
Password	

Website	
User Name	
Password	

Website	
User Name	
Password	

Website	
User Name	
Password	

Notes

WEBSITE PASSWORDS

Website	
User Name	
Password	

Website	
User Name	
Password	

Website	
User Name	
Password	

Website	
User Name	
Password	

Website	
User Name	
Password	

Directions for Completion

Access to your emails will be important for your family as will access to your social media accounts. We always have more social media that we expect. List any accounts you have with:

- Facebook
- Instagram
- Twitter
- Reddit
- TikTok
- Pinterest
- Snapchat

The following list is not exhaustive it is just a start to get you going.

Notes

EMAIL AND SOCIAL MEDIA PASSWORDS

Email Address	
Password	

Email Address	
Password	

Social Media Website	
Username	
Password	

Social Media Website	
Username	
Password	

Social Media Website	
Username	
Password	

Notes

Social Media Website	
Username	
Password	

Social Media Website	
Username	
Password	

Social Media Website	
Username	
Password	

Social Media Website	
Username	
Password	

Social Media Website	
Username	
Password	

Notes

Social Media Website	
Username	
Password	

Social Media Website	
Username	
Password	

Social Media Website	
Username	
Password	

Social Media Website	
Username	
Password	

Social Media Website	
Username	
Password	

Notes

Social Media Website	
Username	
Password	

Social Media Website	
Username	
Password	

Social Media Website	
Username	
Password	

Social Media Website	
Username	
Password	

Social Media Website	
Username	
Password	

Notes

Social Media Website	
Username	
Password	

Social Media Website	
Username	
Password	

Social Media Website	
Username	
Password	

Social Media Website	
Username	
Password	

Social Media Website	
Username	
Password	

Directions for Completion

Not everyone owns firearms, but if you do we have provided a space for you list your collection and any special instructions.

Notes

GUNS

Gun Cabinet Location: _____

Gun Cabinet Key Location: _____

Gun Cabinet Lock Code: _____

Paper Work Location: _____

Type:	
Make:	
Trigger Lock Code:	
Special Instructions:	

Type:	
Make:	
Trigger Lock Code:	
Special Instructions:	

Notes

Type:	
Make:	
Trigger Lock Code:	
Special Instructions:	

Type:	
Make:	
Trigger Lock Code:	
Special Instructions:	

Notes

Notes

Type:	
Make:	
Trigger Lock Code:	
Special Instructions:	

Type:	
Make:	
Trigger Lock Code:	
Special Instructions:	

Notes

Notes

Type:	
Make:	
Trigger Lock Code:	
Special Instructions:	

Type:	
Make:	
Trigger Lock Code:	
Special Instructions:	

Notes

Notes

Notes

Notes

Notes

Notes

Notes

Thank you for purchasing **Important Information for my Family**.
We would love to hear your thoughts, suggestions and opinions.
To do so we encourage you to leave a review on Amazon.

This Book is a companion Book to **Important Information about my Funeral Plan**, a book that contains information your Family will need for your funeral service, it is also available on Amazon.
Scan the QR code at the front of this book to access **Important Information about my Funeral Plan**

Printed in Great Britain
by Amazon

81680956R00082